I know . . .

"It's hard being a manager!

Somebody's got to do it! Why not me?"

I know . . .

"It's hard being a manager!

Somebody's got to do it!
Why not me?"

H.R. Scott

To order additional copies of this book, contact:
Xlibris Corporation
1-888-795-4274
www.Xlibris.com
Orders@Xlibris.com
68537

WHAT'S INSIDE FOR YOUR READING ENJOYMENT

I dedicate this book to my parents

Lela Frances Sanford-Scott and John Henry Scott.

You are always in my thoughts and my prayers!

I love you and I miss you!

INTRODUCTION

I HAVE BEEN asked on several different occasions why I have not written my own book regarding managing. I thought about it over the years as I continued to mentor and educate managers on how to be a better and wiser manager. When one day while flying back to California from my son's graduation, something happened that changed my life forever.

Traveling is tiring and this time was no exception and I fell asleep when suddenly, I awoke feeling nauseated so I decided to go to the restroom in case I had an unexpected moment. As I walked down the aisle, I became dizzy and realized that I was not going to make it. Next thing I knew, I was falling to the floor. Thankfully a few of the passengers caught me going down.

As I lay on the floor, I could hear the passengers talking. Naturally I was confused and I wondered what was going on. Fortunately for me, one of the passengers that caught me was a physician. Everything turned out well. I just needed some cold compresses to the old forehead and within ten minutes, I was back up in my seat. As I sat there, my mind began racing. This type of situation had never happened to me before. It was at that moment that I realized that my life could have ended that day on the plane.

I began to think about my professional career. I don't know why I focused on my career but these were the only thoughts that seemed to give me peace. I thought about how if I'd died, my heart's desires and visions would have been lost forever. It was at this point that I decided it was God that was sending me a message, that I had procrastinated long enough and it was time for me to get this book out and to write it my way.

What is more important to me than anything else is that you get something out of this message. It is intended to have a little humor to it but I want the message to be clear that you benefit and grow as a manager.

"It's hard being a manager. Somebody's got to do it! Why not me?"

IN THE BEGINNING

I REMEMBER THE first time I encountered what it felt like to be a manager. I was 18 years old and I was working as a Messenger at a hospital in Detroit Michigan. After working for one month, my supervisor asked me if I would like to work as the Dispatcher. In this position, the Dispatcher is responsible for taking all of the calls and then assigning a Messenger to perform the pick-up and delivery. Man, I was excited about serving as the Dispatcher. It meant that I would be able to sit all day, give orders, and watch the others do all of the walking.

When my co-workers (who had been working there longer than me) walked into the office and saw me sitting in that Dispatcher's chair, I could see the attitude. When they found out that the supervisor had asked me if I wanted to learn how to be a Dispatcher, they made that one day that should have been such a wonderful memory to me, a day of hell. Every time I gave them an assignment, I got resistance. They purposely delivered the packages to the wrong place. They took extra time on their runs. What would normally take 10-20 minutes ended up taking 40 minutes or more. Complaints started coming into the office. The list got longer and it turned out to be a bad situation. By 1 o'clock. that afternoon, yes the same day I was 'promoted', my supervisor decided to take over and I was taken out of my new and exciting management role.

"How dare my co-workers treat me this way?" I said to myself. I had done nothing to them. I respected each of them. I spoke every morning and held basic conversation. I never talked about them to their peers and respected the type of work mentality they chose to have as a Messenger. I was the same as them. After all, the only title I had like everybody else in that department was Messenger. But I stood out from the rest. Knowing how important time keeping was, I got to work on time, and learned every department in the hospital and how long it would take to get from one point to the other. I knew to call back into the office if I encountered a problem that would interfere with my run time. I went to lunch when assigned and came back on time. I never called into work sick unless it was absolutely necessary. I never complained about any run that was assigned to me. If I felt that a run could be configured differently, I would explain it to my supervisor and respectfully accepted whatever decision she made on my suggestion. I spoke to folks in the various departments and I became known as one of the reliable Messengers.

Yet, because I took pride in my work, conducted myself in good work ethics, and had a positive attitude, I was sabotaged. The experience taught me something very important. I knew that I wanted to be in management and was determined to get there one day. As long ago as that was, regardless of some difficult and challenging times, there are no regrets and this thought remains the same.

"It's hard being a manager. Somebody's got to do it! Why not me?"

WHO IS IN CONTROL?

ONE OF THE first questions I ask managers during management training is who is in control? Are you in control or are your employees in control? It's a bad situation to be in when you have the title manager but you have no power or control. Let me give you a few examples and see if you can relate.

Staff Meetings

You are holding a staff meeting and one of your employees has decided that they are going to control the meeting. They become disruptive, argumentative, they make noises, they make smart comments under their breath or they get up and walk out of the meeting as if what you have to say doesn't mean anything. Hmm, is this you? Now the question is, how do you handle employees who act in this way?

Simple, you maintain in control at all times. Trust me, I know that it's not easy but it must be done. I once had an employee who tried to take over my meeting. She was all of the above and some. I'll tell you how I handled this employee when I finish my thoughts about maintaining control.

There are different approaches you can use to maintain control in your staff meetings or meetings in general where you are serving as the facilitator.

Stop the meeting and focus solely on the employee and ask if there is a problem? You can do so by being diplomatic without losing control and 'shooting straight' and say to the employee,

"Based on how you are behaving today in this meeting, you appear to be angry. Do you have a problem?"

If this doesn't resolve the issue you may want to press in further and become less tolerant or compassionate in what you say, for example,

"This type of behavior will not be tolerated by me. It is my expectation that you will participate in this meeting like the rest of the staff but you will not try to control this meeting. Do we have an understanding?"

The answer should be yes but there are times when the answer will be no, and the employee will continue to act out. At this point, you ask the employee to step into a private room and you tell them how disappointed you are that you had to stop the meeting to address their behavior and that they are not permitted to return to the meeting. You will meet with them separately to provide them with the highlights of the meeting and to discuss performance expectations if they plan to continue working in your department.

Now I will tell you what I did with the employee who tried to take over my meeting with her undesirable disposition. I terminated the employee because she was one week shy of her probationary period. I decided to let her go because if she behaved this way while on a trial period, just, imagine what she may have done once off probation.

Doesn't it feel good to be in control again? If you lose control, employees see that you have allowed one of their peers to take over and you are perceived as weak. Not in control. Remember, good managers always remain in control at least 99% of the time. I know . . .

"It's hard being a manager. Somebody's got to do it! Why not me?"

SNAP-CRACKLE-POP

A S A MANAGER you need to learn the snap-crackle-pop method. This method is for those of you who have a really hard time dealing with adversarial employees. Quite simply, you don't like conflict. It is for those managers who believe there is good in everyone. They try to show everyone respect but because they are so "nice" they are perceived to be weak; you have allowed your employees to be disrespectful and (in many cases) just down right insubordinate embarrassing you on a number of occasions with the insubordinate employee being the topic of conversation at home with your spouse, family and friends. When you see them coming you get angry or you try extremely hard to avoid them. You try to meet with them as little as possible. The bottom line is, you just can't stand them. When does it end?

I had a manager who was in this situation and had been for a long time. I had no idea it was this bad until she told me how miserable an employee was making her work and home life. I told her that I didn't blame the employee for her misery. I blamed her, the manager. The reality of this situation and every situation that a manager has lost control in is this. The manager has allowed the employee to disrupt their world. The employee has been permitted to think that they can say or do whatever they like and you constantly give in to their demands. I suggested to the manager to use a term that I call the snap-crackle-pop method.

The next time this employee comes into your office or attempts to corner you in the hallway –

You SNAP: ask the employee to come in and take a seat.

You CRACKLE: you close the door.

You POP: you sit down in your chair, turn and look the employee in the eyes (and whatever you do don't lose the eye contact) and let them have it.

You tell the employee how you are tired of their foolishness, their bullying and here are your expectations. You end it with a "Do you understand me?"

The manager tried it and the feedback that I got was great. Not only did the employee state that she had no idea her behavior was that bad but she apologized. It turned out to be a win-win situation. The manager asked me what she should have done if the employee became argumentative. I told her the same thing she did the first time which is Snap-Crackle-Pop all over again. After all, she is the manager and ultimately she will win the battle. I know . . .

"It's hard being a manager. Somebody's got to do it! Why not me?"

OPEN DOOR POLICY

I HAVE ASKED managers at numerous training sessions if they have an open door policy. An effective manager knows that they must have an open door policy. Naturally, they will say "yes!" Then the fun begins because I get the chance to ask them a few questions on how they would handle certain situations.

Let's say you are in the middle of a very important project. You waited until the last minute to get the work done, sound familiar?. The clock is your worse enemy right now. Your boss has been asking about the project and today it is due. Yes, you are stressed! There is a knock at the door and it's your employee who would like to have a word with you. How would you handle the situation?

Manager number one said.
"I would ask the employee if it is not urgent, can it wait until I complete this special project."

Manager number two said
"I would tell the employee they will have to get back to me. I am in the middle of a special project."

You are probably thinking that both of these responses to be very good. They are decent responses but I would recommend you respond like this,

"Hi, come on in and have a seat. How are things going? What is on your mind today?

The employee begins to explain why they needed to speak with me. Once they have finished and I have assessed that it is something that can indeed wait until I have completed the project, I then say,

"First, I would like to thank you for bringing this situation to my attention. It is very important that we deal with this issue. Before you stepped in to my office, I was working on a project for my boss. I procrastinated and waited until the last minute to get this project done. Is it alright with you if I finish this project then you and I can meet either later on today or tomorrow to resolve your issue?"

In most cases the employee agrees with my suggestion because they hear and see the respect through my actions as a busy manager that is still prepared to take time to hear from an employee.

The difference between my response and the two examples of the other managers is that it is a "true" open door policy. I made the employee feel important, empowered and I allowed the employee to see that even I (as the manager) fall behind sometimes. I gave the person what so many employees need, just a little respect.

The problem with the responses of the other two managers is that manager number one sent a clear message that, "I am busy but if I have to talk to you I will." Manager number two sent a clear message of, "I am the boss and right now, you are not important."

Remember, it is the responsibility of the manager to always take the time to make the employee feel their worth. So, when you say you have an open door policy, make sure that it really is an open door. I know . . .

"It's hard being a manager. Somebody's got to do it! Why not me?"

It is very important to me that you do not get bored while reading this book. So, I purposely jump to different topics to keep you wanting to read more. So, do not look for a particular structure because you won't find it. Now enjoy!

I AM FOCUSED ON YOU

AS A YOUNG and new manager, I used to have employees who just refused to do what they needed to do. I would look at their work productivity and say to myself, "Is it live or Memorex?" In other words, I knew that the employee knew how to do their job function. I would ask the employee if everything was alright and inquire as to whether or not there was anything going on preventing them from performing their job function. I would always get back the same response that everything was fine and no problems. The next thing I know and I've started making excuses for the employee. Yes, I was creating excuses as to why they were unable to complete the job function which was the first stages of loss of control that could easily have led to an abusive situation.

I continued to call the employee into my office to bring to their attention about their low performance. I will never forget the day when the employee said to me, "I feel that you are harassing me. I am doing this job to the best of my ability and I don't appreciate being singled out." It was amazing to me as to how this employee took my concerns and turned them on me making me feel like I had done something wrong.

I went home that evening with my mind on that employee and what he had said to me. I remember saying to myself, "I need to get focused on this guy asap." The next day, I called him back into my office. I told him that I was disappointed that he felt that I was harassing him and that I'd had time to think about what he said and rather than call him back into my office on a daily basis, I was letting him know that I was focused on him. Naturally he asked me what that meant. I was happy to explain that it meant I was watching his every move. His attendance, work performance, and work productivity. I also explained that if he showed no improvement in these areas,

I would document the results and that once I had gathered enough documentation that he would be sure to feel the end result. Again, he asked me what that meant, so I made it clear and told him, "In time, you will understand." The employee walked out of my office with an attitude and I sat there with a smile on my face.

Being focused on an employee, means that, I am on a mission. As a manager, I have to be sure that the work is done in a timely manner, therefore, if each team member does their share, the company will thrive, so I make certain that I watch every single move this and every attitudinal employee makes. If there is no improvement it is only right to terminate them but without documentation I cannot substantiate this type of decision. The other employees could see that the manager was clearly focused on him, and interestingly, they did nothing wrong for me to focus on them. Knowing that association brings about assimilation, the other employees began to socialize less with him. Don't ask me what happened but the employee's performance improved greatly and he worked very hard to maintain his work productivity just like his co-workers. A few months went by and I called him into my office to tell him that I was no longer focused on him and how proud I was of how he increased his performance and how it positively impacted his productivity. The employee gave me a big smile and admitted that he was wrong. He ultimately turned out to be one of my best employees.

After this experience, anytime an employee begins to fall down in their performance and after meeting with them, if I discover that it is another attitudinal employee that doesn't care, I simply call them into my office and let them know how I am focused on them. They always ask their co-workers what this means.

The response from the co-workers is always the same, "you'll see if you don't straighten up." I know . . .

"It's hard being a manager. Somebody's got to do it! Why not me?"

DO YOU SPEAK?

I CANNOT BEGIN to tell you how often I heard employees say, "Why should I work harder, my manager doesn't speak to me anyway." Does this sound familiar to you? Are you one of those managers who feel that they do not have to speak to their employees? If so, you really need to read this section.

How can you possibly think that as a manager you do not have to speak to your employees, EVERY MORNING! I just don't understand the mentality of any person who claims to be a manager and does not speak.

I can clearly remember managers who I've reported for not speaking to me. It offended and upset me. Once I realized how moody or foolish they really were, I didn't work hard to make them look good at all and decided to do the bare minimum. I would see them speak to other people and I realized, for whatever reason, they had their favorite employees:; I was not one of the "golden children." From this experience I vowed that if I ever rose to a leadership level where I could have an impact on other managers, I would stress the importance of speaking to the staff.

Everybody wants to feel important! When you say, good morning or hello to your employee, in most cases, they really do appreciate it. As an example, I was working as the Director of Human Resources for a small company that had around 150 employees. Everyday, I would take the time to speak to as many employees as possible. I can remember going from one floor to the other, simply saying good morning or asking how they were doing. I could tell that the employees enjoyed seeing me and I enjoyed spending that short moment with them when one day, I had something on my mind and I walked by an employee and did not speak. The employee said to me, "So you are not speaking this morning Mr. Scott. Don't tell me that you are going to start acting like my manager." Not only did I apologize but I told them that I had a lot on my mind with the new owners of the company making many changes. I remember thanking the employee for reminding me that it doesn't matter what's on my mind, as the manager, the employee always comes first.

If you want employees to be loyal, hard working, respectful and to trust you, it begins with speaking to them. Get to know your employees. Try to find out little tidbits about their life and what is important to them. Let them know that you care about who they are. Don't start speaking to certain employees and others you just walk by as if they don't exist. That is wrong! A good manager will make every employee feel special. If you work in an area that has thousands of employees, you can still speak. When I walk through the hospitals that I am responsible for overseeing, because of the name badges, I am able to speak to everybody, There really is no excuse for poor communication. The word that I hear back on me is that, I am very nice, *"he always speaks and acknowledges my presence"*. This is what I do, and I believe every good manager should try to do the same thing. I know . . .

"It's hard being a manager. Somebody's got to do it! Why not me?"

IMAGE

D URING CHRISTMAS TIME one year, an employee came up to me and told me about the Christmas party at his manager's house. He told me that he had a great time and they partied almost the entire night. Then he told me they had smoked marijuana as well. I asked him if the manager had known that they had smoked marijuana at his home. He told me the manager was the one who provided the marijuana. I was shocked! When I approached the manager I asked him if what the employee told me was true. He stated that he was in the privacy of his own home and he could do what he wanted to do during off hours. I was shocked and surprised that the manager confirmed the employee's story. Well, the manager was terminated from his position.

What makes any manager think that their role stops at 5:00 pm or whenever they leave to go home? Being a manager is something that you do 24 hours a day, 7 days a week. That's right! I did not utter, mutter or stutter because being a manager is something that you do 24 hours a day, 7 days a week. It is a commitment! When you ask to be hired as a manager you are committing to stand apart, give more, work harder, work smarter, and to portray an image that reflects you as part of the bigger picture, the company you represent.

When employees invite you to their home for parties or other functions, you must use wisdom. If you get to the house and you walk in and smell drugs or see drugs, you should have the common sense to leave. Tell the employee that you are not comfortable in that environment. If you see that the behavior of the guest is so foolish, you need to excuse yourself. Why? Because if you engage in foolishness, you lose respect and I assure you that this will happen in a spiraling, out of control way. The employee goes into work and tells everybody what you did and said at the party. Your employees will know what you drank, if you danced, if you used inappropriate language, if you tried to talk to someone romantically, and the list goes on. The focus is on you.

You can go to a function of your employees and enjoy yourself. But remember that you are still responsible for mentoring and managing this person. Do not make the fatal mistake like the manager in the example I gave you. You cannot manage people and try to be their friend as well. It's like when I tell my children. I am not trying to be your friend, I am your father. I never confuse the two because the day any of my children try to speak to me the way they speak to their friends, we now have a problem.

Don't be so naïve as to think that employees don't talk about their managers quite a bit, they absolutely do. Yes, you are part of their daily conversation because you are their manager. Employees respect you until you have done something to cause them to disrespect you. Don't damage your image. I know . . .

"It's hard being a manager. Somebody's got to do it! Why not me?"

WHY I RECOMMEND YOU BE REMOVED FROM YOUR MANAGEMENT POSITION

YES, DURING MY human resource career, I've had to remove managers from their position. Let me explain why and I believe you will agree that I did the right thing.

I have worked for five major organizations during which time I have learned from others and my own mistakes, so if I allow you insight and reveal a situation that is a problem to me, it should be for you too.

The day I start in a new position, is how I intend to continue. Adopt the policy, "Start how you mean to go on." I have found this to be the start of a healthy, productive employment. At the first opportunity, I take the time to meet each of the managers and ask them basic questions about their respective departments. This is a very good indicator on the manager's effectiveness. The first sign for me that a manager may not be effective and I know that there's a problem is when I ask for them to tell me about their department and they are unable to explain the department's purpose and or the functions of each of their employees to me. Don't let me find out that they have been managing the department for years.

Next I begin to watch the behavior of the manager and assess if they are professional and are acting with a management demeanor. This doesn't mean walking around as if you are better than everyone else. It means you are modeling the behavior of how you expect your employees to behave.

Here is an outline of the areas I look at and stress to you that are being observed about you as a manager.

- Time keeping – Ask yourself – If you are late for work, why do you expect your employees to be on time?
- Attitude – Are you speaking to everyone and showing them respect?
- Attendance record – Are you calling in ill excessively?
- Skill application – Are you encouraging your employees and providing training and development?
- Communication – Are the memos and other documents you send out written well? When you give a presentation, are you prepared regarding the subject matter?
- Image – Do you dress professionally? Do you wear your hair professionally?

Relax a little and don't worry or think that you will be terminated if you fail any of the above. The next step is to begin to work with you and bring to your attention those areas where you are lacking. Once these concerns have been brought to your attention and you fail to correct them, then it is time to consider moving you into a position that is better suited for your skill set. I know it sounds cold but it is reality. Corporations (especially the corporations of today) don't have time for foolishness. Managers are earning very hefty salaries and other perks and so you are expected to represent them accordingly. It is the expectation of the senior leadership that you will produce and function according to all that money they are paying you. If you don't want to, then I know they can find somebody who will gladly do it in place of you. I know . . .

"It's hard being a manager. Somebody's got to do it! Why not me?"

CONFLICT

WITHOUT A DOUBT, as a manager you will deal with conflict at some point in time in your career. I have seen more managers' struggle with conflict than any other area of management. If you do not like dealing with confrontation or (to make it sound better) bring performance or attendance issues to people, you should not consider the world of management.

I joined a company as the Director of Human Resources. The day I met with the management staff they talked about the poor attendance of their employees, nasty behavior, poor work ethics, etc. They wanted me (the new HR Director) to clean everything up and to get their employees on the right track. After everybody finished talking about their problems, I told them that the first problem I'd identified was management itself. None of them had been doing their jobs. The employees are the way they are because management was afraid of dealing with conflict. (Who is in control?) They got upset with me. I could see the attitude on their faces and I could hear it in their responses to me. But, I knew that I was right. Any time employees are that out of control you can only look at management. Look at it this way. A country, a State, a county, a city, a town, a village and a family are all organized on a hierarchical basis, therefore, if the top of the tree gets messed up or misses their purpose, there will, because it is unavoidable for it not to, have a *"knock on"* effect further down the tree. It starts and finishes at the top. I know . . .

"It's hard being a manager. Somebody's got to do it! Why not me?"

JUGGLING TOO MANY BALLS

A S THE MANAGER, it can appear that you are seen as the dumping ground. Everything is dumped in your lap. When there is a new policy, you are the one who has to enforce it. When the employees don't complete their work, you are the one who has to get it done. If the budget isn't right, you are the one who has to figure out why. Yes, the position of manager is seen as the dumping ground.

So, how does one manage all of these tasks and problems that have been dumped in your lap? Let me tell you about one of my situations and how I handled it. This just might help you.

I worked at a medical center in Detroit, Michigan back in 1993. One day, they had a massive lay off. They had everybody who worked in administration and Human Resources sit in this huge conference room and at five minute intervals the phone would ring and someone was asked to step across the hall. The more I think about it, it was one of the worse layoffs I have ever experienced. By the time they had finished, twenty folks had been laid off in the HR Department. That only left five of us to get the work done of twenty five people. It was crazy! We'd been cut by over three quarters and were trying to meet the same deadlines as usual. Out of the five of us who were left, one developed an ulcer another had to increase her high blood pressure medicine whilst one cried about how she could not take it any longer and the last one was smoking at least two packs of cigarettes per eight hours. To get the work done, all of them (and notice I said all of them) worked a minimum of 12 hours per day starting as early as 5:00 am every morning.

Remember, I stress, "them", not me. I started work at 8:00am and left everyday at 5:00pm. Why? Because I knew there was no way that I could meet all of those deadlines and maintain a healthy personal life. At that time, I was married with two children and I was the primary provider. My children were very young and they needed to see their father and spend quality time together. Then, one of my co-workers noticed that I was not working as hard as them. She approached me and asked me how was it that they were working long hours but I was working the same hours prior to the layoff? I told her that I have a strategy for juggling all of these priorities.

This was my strategy:

- I listed each task that was given to me.
- Once listed, I prioritized them accordingly.
- Once prioritized, I took the top one and assessed how long it would take me to do this particular job and how often I had to do it.
- I also assessed the negative impact it would have on the organization if I did not get it done.
- Based on my calculations, I was only able to perform seven out of twenty tasks on a daily basis, this meant I could not complete the other thirteen tasks. Knowing this, I sent an email to my superior and told him that I'd ranked my priorities and the reasons why. I then asked him *"If there is something you would like for me to do different or reprioritize what I have shown you, please let me know. If not, I will continue to work on what I have identified as priority and if I get the opportunity, I will try to work on the other thriteen tasks."* The response I got back was for me to work on what I listed as priority and keep up the good work.

My co-worker looked at me in amazement. Why? because she never thought to do what I had done. Not only had I prioritized my own work, but I had supporting documentation from my superior approving what I had done. Let's keep this real. There is only so much work you can handle. A good manager will let their superior know when they are overwhelmed with work. When this occurs, it is important to prioritize and enjoy what you love to do. I know . . .

"It's hard being a manager. Somebody's got to do it! Why not me?"

MANAGEMENT AND LABOR

I COULD WRITE an entire book about the relationship between management and labor. However, this book isn't about labor only. So, here is my take as it relates to this topic.

The organization I work for is based in Northern California. This organization has developed a strong relationship with labor called, a partnership. When I first joined the company, I found this partnership to be very interesting and healthy for the organization because the two entities (labor and management) trusted and respected each other enough to form the partnership.

As I began to meet the management group and listen to their concerns centered on labor, I quickly realized that there was a *"disconnect"*. What was so interesting is that, the disconnect, was not with the labor side but with the management side. What management had failed to do was read and understand the union contracts. In my meetings with management, I would ask how many of them had a copy of the labor contract. Very few hands would go up. Then I asked how many of them had a copy of the contract but never read it. Quite a few hands went up. So, if you don't have a copy of the contract and or if you have a copy and you never read it, how then, can you work effectively in a labor environment?

Immediately, we began to make labor training mandatory for management. In the past, management only attended labor training if they could find the time. The end result was that a high number of managers were trying to manage a labor group based on non labor practices. This combination created nothing but a pile of grievances and bitter relationships between the two groups.

You as the manager represent the organization overall, it is therefore your responsibility to read, understand and respect the union contract. I am not suggesting that you memorize the entire contract. However, you should familiarize yourself with certain segments covering issues that may come up on a regular basis such as the sections on attendance, discipline, transfers, promotions, etc. It is foolish to think that you can manage or discipline or make any changes with labor employees if you don't know the do's and the don'ts. I constantly hear labor talk about how management is not familiar with their contract. It makes you look bad as a manager and as if you don't care about what is important to them which in turn will cause for lack of respect and so the disintegration of the relationship commences.

I enjoy working with labor because they only ask that you treat their members fair and with dignity. I know there are some unions that believe in the "old" traditional way of doing things which is to be hostile, angry and disrespectful. I believe however that this "method" of management results in a less than productive workforce. As I stressed earlier, it is important to build a relationship between management and labor without crossing the line of losing respect of the employee through being 'too friendly' and then to be perceived as weak. In the "partnership" relationship there is a healthy participation and balance based on everyone knowing, understanding and respecting where the "line" is. All relationships take time to develop, this can only be done through trust and setting boundaries. With the experience I have in the organization I am with at present they have a great management-labor relationship and as a human resource professional, I am enjoying what they have established – labor plus management equal partnership. I know . . .

"It's hard being a manager. Somebody's got to do it! Why not me?"

REPORTING RELATIONSHIPS

T HIS SHOULD BE a very interesting segment for you. I need you to identify which of these types of bosses you report to:

The, Control Freak
The, I Will Not Support You Publicly
The, Ultimate

I bet you are smiling right now as you think about which of these personalities belong to your boss. If you identify more than two, I suggest you look for another job immediately!

Starting with the, "Control Freak" boss.

Yes, I worked for a "Control Freak" but without a mentor to help me work this 'relationship' out I had to find out the hard way and it took a while for me to understand why they turned out this way.

My "Control Freak" boss would give me an assignment to do and ask that I bring it to her before submission. Each and every time, she would make massive changes to the assignment. I used to say to myself, "*If this is how you wanted it, why didn't you just do it yourself?*" When I made a suggestion based on what they wanted me to do, I would get the attack response. This is the type of response that make you shut your mouth up immediately because you are in a no win situation. Once you make all of the proposed changes, you are told that you are going to report out at the meeting. You get into the meeting and as you start to talk about the report, your "Control Freak" boss takes over and gives the entire presentation and as well as this, when it's time for questions and answers your "Control Freak" boss responds to every question. You can see the looks on the other folk's faces in the room and you feel humiliated. After the meeting, your "Control Freak" boss calls you into the office and tells you that you did a great job and keep up the good work. Yet, everyone else is asking you, *"How can you work with that "Control Freak?"*

This is how I handled my time with my "Control Freak" boss. I quickly realized what it was I had to do to keep her happy, in this case it was simple enough. When I was given an assignment, my role was to provide the basic outline of everything. It didn't matter that I knew that she was going to change the bulk of what I provided, what mattered was that I did my job. Even when I was asked to facilitate a meeting, knowing that she would take over the meeting didn't prevent me from preparing for it, I did this for two reasons. I was fulfilling my job requirements and I was always prepared to present the information in case she was absent or called into another meeting. Knowing that I could not change this person, nor was it my position to do so, helped and I maintained a professional, personable, yet non personal relationship with her.

So, I became comfortable with the role of serving as her "Assistant" (even though I had a much higher title). As long as I continued to get adequate increases, I was satisfied. Did I learn anything? Yes! That I would never function as a control freak nor did I want to be seen as one. I know . . .

"It's hard being a manager. Somebody's got to do it! Why not me?"

Moving on to the, "I Will Not Support You Publicly" boss.

My "I Will Not Support You Publicly" boss was very interesting. I remember when I joined this particular company and everything appeared to be going fine. My boss had called me into her office and was complaining about a process and that she wanted me to bring it up at the next meeting. Trusting my new boss with all of the leaders in the company, I brought up the topic. It was interesting because once I brought the topic up, the room got quiet. The top man looked at me and he began to beat me down and more or less chastise me for bringing up the topic. He said that everyone knew the financial implications and I should have done my homework prior to the meeting. I felt so bad. I looked at my boss and she said nothing. As a matter of fact, she joined in with the Chair and made me look even more like a fool. I was furious. I could feel the heat swelling up in my head. My heart started racing more. My palms started sweating and here I was in my first meeting and I was made to look like a fool. After the meeting, I went into my boss' office and asked her what just happened. She tried to act as if she had no idea that I would have gotten attacked in that manner, apologized and changed the subject.

As I began to get to know my peers better, they welcomed me to the club of "Don't look for support." She'd done the same thing to them and this was why there was such a high turnover of management in her area. Did I learn anything? Yes! This is the worst type of boss to work for if you ask me. You never know if they will attack or support you and with an undetermined response, this can add to the stress and undermine your performance. What I had to learn and I recommend you do too is accept all results are good and serve for the purpose of making you a "better" manager. I know . . .

"It's hard being a manager. Somebody's got to do it! Why not me?"

Finally and with relief we have the "Ultimate" boss.

The "Ultimate" boss is one of the best leaders one can ever report to and enjoy their leadership. I have been given the opportunity to work with several ultimate bosses. What makes them ultimate is how they allow you the ability to do your job. They don't try to over power you, control you, deny you or disrespect you. These individuals let you do exactly what you were hired to do and provide you with excellent guidance and leadership.

When I was working at this one organization, they were looking for a CEO. All of the various leaders were allowed to interview the candidates except for me. I was not upset because I had just gotten hired and I was still in my learning curve (an excuse that I made up for them). The truth is, I really didn't understand why I had not been allowed to participate. When the CEO came on board, I remember the day I met him. Somewhere in the conversation, he asked me why I had not been a part of the interview team. I told him that I had no idea. He then asked me why I was not participating in organizational decisions like my peers. Again, my only response was I didn't know. Next thing I knew, I was being told that my office would be moving next door to the CEO's.

This ultimate leader knew that in order for the organization to be successful, he needed human resource management at the leadership table. He allowed me to use my skills and knowledge in ways that it would take too long to explain, needless to say, whenever he moved his office, my office was always positioned next to him. He asked for my opinion and in almost every situation used the advice I gave him. He took my leadership to another level. He always complimented my human resource skills and knowledge. He allowed me to attend any conference or workshop without hesitation. He got me involved in financial projects that enhanced my finance skills greatly. In return, I gave him what he asked me to do. He received outstanding human resource performance from me and my staff.

This is what I call an ultimate boss because they help to bring the ultimate performance out of their employees. I can only hope that you can experience working for someone like him the way I did. I know . . .

"It's hard being a manager. Somebody's got to do it! Why not me?"

YOU THE PSYCHIATRIST

MANAGERS HAVE TO act like a psychiatrist everyday on the job. There is no way we can get around it. Think about it. We have no idea what type of evening our employees have when they leave work. In this day and time, I'm sure that most of the employees go home to stress, being defined as whatever keeps you up at night, and madness.

Our employees have so many pressures on them, that by the time they come to work, we as managers have no idea what mental illness they and therefore, we are dealing with on a daily basis. The question becomes, how do you deal with these issues and still manage them effectively?

What I have done is to remember that we all have issues. When I decided to go into the world of management, it meant that my issues had to come last. My employees came first. When I recognized a performance issue, a bad attitude, poor attendance, verbal outbreaks, non responsive behavior etc. it alerts me to know that something is wrong. Do your homework and investigate.

I have heard managers say to me they have found that often their employees don't want to tell you what is going on with them. I have heard employees say they don't trust management and they don't feel that you care anyway. This type of thinking could only come from how they have been treated by you. If you never showed your staff any empathy, naturally they won't think that you care. If you rarely speak or don't speak at all, why would they want to talk to you about their issues? Remember, relationships take time to build. It is up to you to try to find out and assist them to the best of your ability. However, if they continue to shut down on you, remember most organizations have an Employee Assistance Program (EAP) for you to refer them to for help. Most EAP staff are trained licensed Social Workers who are capable of reaching employees when you can't as a manager. I know . . .

"It's hard being a manager. Somebody's got to do it! Why not me?"

ARE YOU THE PARENT
OR THE MANAGER?

I CANNOT TELL you how many times I have told managers, "You are not their parent. You are their manager!" Sometimes, I believe that as we get older, we begin to look at employees as our children. This is the worst mistake you can make.

I have met managers who have allowed their employees to have bad attendance. The employees come into work late on a regular basis, they take a lot of time off work and dress sloppy, all without discipline. It bothered me to see how he had such a poor attitude but I chose not to intervene because if the manager is happy, why should I let it bother me? The day came when I witnessed this manager extremely upset. I asked what was wrong. She told me that she wanted to write this employee up for poor attendance. I was quite surprised because she always allowed this employee to, *"do his thing."* She then told me that she was informed by his co-workers that on the day he was a no call/no show, she'd asked her employees to call and make sure that he was alright. The response she got back from his co-workers was a message that was quite shocking. He told his co-workers that he was not interested in what she wanted and he wished that she'd stop calling him. (I choose not to use the exact words that he used but trust me they were so foul that I could see the pain in her face).

I did not allow the manager to write this employee up; there is a process that has to be followed before you can do so and it had not been met, so I told her that because she treated this employee as if he was one of her children, she failed to follow the documented process and the employee had placed her in a bad situation leaving her very angry.

It is important that you recognize that most employees will take advantage of you when they recognize that you are treating them like one of your children. Depending on how long this, 'relationship' has been developing, you may call them, "baby" or you tell them, "you remind me of my child." How about, "I am just trying to protect you." All of these comments are inappropriate and could lead to problems. I have seen these employees turn on their managers and accuse them of harassment. Try not to let yourself fall into this type of management style. Your employees are not your children! You were hired to manage them and to do so effectively. I know . . .

"It's hard being a manager. Somebody's got to do it! Why not me?"

YOUR APPEARANCE MATTERS

I DON'T CARE what anyone says, your appearance matters especially, if you are in management. I always wear a shirt and tie into work. Call it the old school way but it's what I believe is the best way for me to look representing my organization. I have the mindset that I never know when I may get called into a meeting. I believe that managers must always be prepared. Employees have asked me my entire career why I wear a suit everyday to work. My response is and continues to be that as part of the management team, I must always be prepared for the unexpected. They understand my response and I continue to send a message to employees that I am the manager.

Employees have told me in meetings how their managers will pull them into the office and talk about how inappropriate they are dressed yet they wear the same (if not worse) outfits. It's the *"pot can't talk about the kettle"* concept. I do realize that certain work environments are so relaxed that everybody comes into work dressed extremely casual. I know the philosophy is that if you make the work environment "comfortable" for the employee, they will be happier and be more productive. Professional dress sends a message and as the manager, it is our responsibility to send the right message to our employees. We are after all, acting as a leader and setting an example in leadership. I know . . .

"It's hard being a manager. Somebody's got to do it! Why not me?"

TO THE POTENTIAL EMPLOYEE

I ADDED THIS section because I want potential employees to know that your appearance matters as well. Somewhere, our society has sent the wrong message to potential employees telling them that it doesn't matter how you look or what you wear; it shouldn't have a bearing on whether or not you get hired for the job.

- What makes a potential employee think that an employer wants to have them around their customers who look as if they have just rolled out of bed? This disheveled look and the following, "images" need to be read and taken into consideration by you as the potential employee.

- The increase in visible tattoos can stop someone from hiring you. I look at the potential employee and I see tattoos on their necks, ears, hands, lips, legs, etc. Ask yourself this question. Why would any decent organization want to have you greeting their customers when you look scary? It's not that I'm against tattoos but I know that too many visible ones will hinder you from getting a job.

- Body piercing is not a crime but if you who have pierced your face to the point that you do look scary, this may hinder you in getting that job you had your heart set on. Imagine that you are in a hospital bed and in comes someone who looks like they are out of a science fiction movie. The bulk of our society is elderly and it can be a bit overwhelming for them as well as for young children when approached by an individual with a *"scary look"*. I offer no apology for what I have said I am just keeping it real.

Are you one of those young men who walk into an employment office with their pants hanging down, wearing a shirt three times its normal size, sporting a hat turned around backwards or a scarf tied around your head, have unkempt dreads with the tips dyed blonde, red, auburn or blue? Or are you the young lady dressed in a blouse that exposes too much flesh? What message are you giving out about yourself?

With 25 years of experience in human resources for six different (major) organizations, I am in a position to say this. If you don't change the way you look and dress, your window of opportunity will continue to shrink. Just take the time to look at yourself in the mirror and you decide how you look in your own eyes as much as the eyes of a potential employer. Take the time to appreciate what the workforce, that are your potential peers of that company, are wearing as they get to or leave work and compare it to what you had in mind for the interview or to appreciate why it is you are being passed by for promotion.

As a potential employee now read what I would have to say to a manager looking to hire.

If you don't tune yourself in to every aspect of this potential employee, you will hire the wrong person. Not only should you be looking at how they are dressed but the way they speak. If you can't understand a word they are saying, this may not be the person to bring on board. Be vigilant in all aspects of the interview. Is the application filled out so poorly with misspelled words that you sit there and say to yourself, *"what is going on?"* Don't fool yourself as a potential employee. It will hurt your chances of getting hired. I know . . .

"It's hard being a manager. Somebody's got to do it! Why not me?"

HIRING THE WRONG PERSON

A S A MANAGER, there will come a time when you hire the wrong person to work for you. Don't let it stress you out. There are some people who are professional interviewees. They know what to say and how to say it. They have all of the right moves and you find yourself falling deeper into their trap. You decide to hire the person and suddenly you begin to see behavior that was not noticeable during the interview. You begin to ask yourself why you did not see this character flaw when interviewing. Guess what? It's alright! We all make mistakes and when hiring employees this no exception. The question becomes, can you avoid hiring the wrong person? The answer is, no, you cannot. Your responsibility as a manager is to remember that in most organizations there is a term called "the introductory period" or the "probationary period" and providing you have the right documentation to support a termination, you can only learn through such a mistake.

It is important that when you hire new employees, you must be extremely focused on them with set criteria for you to meet that the new employee's progress can be documented and appreciated at a glance. Then, if they begin to come into work late, even with all the other responsibilities you have to fulfill, you will immediately appreciate this is a sign that you may have a potential attendance problem and act on it there and then. I can't tell you how many times a manager had to jump through hoops to terminate an employee who has bad attendance because they allowed them to get past their probationary period. What makes it even worse is when we look back at their attendance record and we can see the patterns of poor attendance that was ignored. As a manager, you must recognize this behavior and release the employee appropriately which may take time when your company is not in the position to "carry" your oversight.

Likewise, when you ask the employee to perform a function and you clearly see an attitude, they put this look on their face that sends a message of *"how dare you ask me to do something different."* (I call this the non verbal attitude) this is a clear sign of poor work ethics and a bad attitude. It's not about saying to yourself, *"this person is having a bad day"*, or *"this person is on an probationary period and we need to give them time"*. As a manager, you must recognize this behavior and discipline it, or indeed, release the employee appropriately.

There's always the employee when asked to do something a specific way who decides to do it their way. You question your own direction as you think that maybe you were not clear so you ask them (again) to do it a certain way, and (again) they do it their way. This is a clear sign that this employee has a problem taking directions which could cause you serious problems. This is a newly hired employee who does not know the company. You are trying to provide them with the appropriate training and guidance and they insist upon not listening to you. They decide to do it their way and ignore your directive. This is not a good sign. As a manager, you must recognize this behavior and take appropriate action.

These are just a few examples of how important it is for you as a manager to pay close attention to newly hired employees in order to detect and release that employee once you realize you have hired the wrong person. I know . . .

"It's hard being a manager. Somebody's got to do it! Why not me?"

TIDBITS

for managers to think about during their career:

PRESENTATIONS

Have you ever *"phased out"* during a meeting because it is so boring? There is a type of presentation that I know can send the most inspired to sleep. It is when the facilitator is reading word for word what they are presenting. It is important that you remember that everyone in that room is probably degreed and they can read as well. What you should do is to highlight what you are reporting and speak only to those points that you want them to focus on. When you keep your head down and read or have a power point presentation and read, you can lose the attention of your audience. Remember, study what you have to present. Practice your presentation prior to presenting it. Have your own, *"cheat sheet"* to keep you focused, and show them why you are the manager.

ON DUTY

Management is a 24/7 function. I know there are some of you out there who believe that once you get off work, your job ends. Not true from my perspective. When I see employees in the malls, supermarkets and other places, I am still seen as their manager and they introduce me to their friends and family members as their manager. It is important that you remember that your image follows you wherever you go. So now you are thinking, when can you relax? You can relax when you are in places that can only be viewed by certain people. It seems unfair but it's the price we pay when we want to be a manager.

KEEPING YOUR DISTANCE I

Be careful hiring a friend of a friend. Often these situations can turn into a nightmare because if the friend of a friend does not work out, you will feel the repercussions. The friend will call your friend and your friend will begin to tell them the issues and things about you. (Does this sound like a soap opera?) Next thing you know, the friend of your friend is back at work telling everybody what your friend has told them about you. Now you are upset with your friend for telling their friend about your personal business. In the end, you lose your friend and have to look at their friend and you always regret that you ever hired a friend of a friend. Whew! The best thing to do is when someone approaches you about helping a friend, refer them to the Employment Office. Stay out of it!

KEEPING YOUR DISTANCE II

Managers enter into a physical relationship with their employees all of the time. In my opinion, it is one of the worst decisions you can make. I cannot tell you how many times these relationships turn into nightmares for both parties. Once the love is gone, the madness begins. The employee accuses the manager of sexual harassment and it gets to the point that you don't know who is telling the truth. The best advice that I can give to you is to stay away from these types of relationships. Every now and then, a relationship can turn into a fairy tale story. However, the bulk of the ones that I have seen end up in demotions and or termination for both parties.

TRAINING REGIME

It is important that you continue to build your knowledge base as it relates to your profession. The best way to learn about the latest trends in your field is to attend professional conventions related to the position you hold and the company you work for. I attend the professional human resource conventions as often as I can. To interact with others in my profession is important. Through conventions you quickly learn that you are not alone and you will appreciate that the same problems and issues you deal with on a daily basis are universal in all work environments. Through conventions, you can network, build strong professional relationships and, if it is what you want, seek a new job. Ask your employer if they will pay for you to attend these conventions. I support them so much that if the employer says that it is not in the budget, I pay for it myself and recommend that you do to respecting the fact that these organizations have to put together agendas and pay for speakers to come talk about certain topics. They need your support. Based on me being a Human

Resource professional, I recommend to all of you who are in the same profession to go to SHRM, ASHHRA or NAAAHR conventions. It is worth it!

MEETINGS I – Can I Have A Word?

When an employee comes to you and ask that the meeting be confidential, there are few questions you need to ask before you say yes. If the meeting is about another person, it's not fair or professional to allow one employee to talk about another employee without them being present. If it's about a personal issue that has compliance implications with the organization, it cannot be confidential. A good example is if the employee states they are having an affair with someone in management or a co-worker. So remember, when an employee knocks on your door and first thing they ask is can you keep it confidential, ask the right questions.

MEETINGS II – We – vs – You

A good way to build a stronger bond with an employee is when you discover they have done something wrong. As an example, they provided you with a report and in the process of you presenting the report to your boss you realize the information is incorrect. When the meeting is over and you pull the employee back into your office to discuss what happened, always start out with, we. "When I presented your report, I discovered that the numbers were wrong. We should have gone over this report a second time. Next time we will be ready." "As the team commented on your report, I told them that we felt that it was important to add this information." "During the meeting, we really got beat up and this is the reason why. We just did not see this coming." Do you see how I focused on the *"we"* versus *"you"*? Through being diplomatic, the employee will feel the support and will become (in most cases) more loyal than you can imagine.

HONESTY

Know when to say, "I don't know." There is nothing wrong with letting someone know that you don't know. Acting like you know what you don't know can get you into trouble. It can make you look real bad, especially, if there is someone in the room who really knows the answer. Just know when to say, *"I don't know but give me an opportunity to look into it."* Now, that's a person who knows what to do.

I know . . .

"It's hard being a manager. Somebody's got to do it! Why not me?"

NIGHTMARES

I WISH THAT I could tell you that your professional working life will only be full of fun, adventure and fulfillment. There are a small percentage of you who will enjoy this type of career ladder. These are the folks who start out with a company at an early age and retire as a senior leader with forty years of service. They may have experienced a few bumps along the way but ultimately they were given the right opportunities with the right support.

But for some of you, it will be a nightmare. My career nightmares are ones that I will never forget. I know that we are told you have to let it go and move on. It is easy to move on but, for some of us it can take a little longer to let it go. It's like everything else in life, we are a product of our past; experiences good or bad are a part of our historical memory.

The reason why I am talking about career nightmares is because I have listened to numerous managers tell me about unfair treatment. I have watched the tears rolling down their faces. I have heard the pain in their voices and my heart goes out to them because I have been where they are.

Nightmare 1

My first nightmare boss gave me the worse assignments and to add insult to injury, when I decided to leave the department, blocked every promotion I tried to get. The end result of this nightmare is that I ultimately found another position. But let's take a positive look at something here. Why did my manager block me? Was it because I was good at what I did and he wanted to keep me on or was I so bad that he was trying to punish me and maintain management over me? The situation for me was stagnant and I needed to move on, eventually of course this did happen, but the process of being able to was most challenging.

Nightmare 2

My second nightmare boss criticized every single assignment I submitted. At first, you look at yourself and wonder if it's you. One of my co-workers was convinced that I was being paranoid. So, we switched the names on our reports. The report with my name on it was highly criticized. Our boss said it was one of the worse summations ever. The report that had my co-workers name on it was highly praised as being outstanding work. My co-worker was in shock. This was good for me in many ways, ultimately it built me up and I was able to move on to greener pastures.

Nightmare 3

My third nightmare boss gave me assignments with deadline dates that were impossible to meet. So, each time I met with this person it was what I call, *"beat me up time"*. They could not understand why I was not meeting my deadlines. Each time I had solid proof as to why I could not meet the deadline, they said that I was making excuses. The end result, I was reassigned to report to someone else.

I need you to understand the ultimate outcome from all three of these nightmare situations.

"THESE MANAGERS WERE TERMINATED BASED ON THEIR POOR MANAGEMENT AND INTERPERSONAL STYLES."

Yes, all three of them were ultimately terminated. The message is that you cannot be a successful manager and manage people if you develop management behaviors like these individuals. Eventually, these styles will catch up with you. Someone higher up will begin to hear about your inappropriate management style and do to you what you have done to others. It starts and ends at the top.

These management styles are the types that generate lawsuits called harassment, unfair treatment or discrimination. If you implement any of these types of management styles, it is unfair to an organization to hire or promote you into a management position. In the long run, it will cost the organization thousands of dollars in legal fees especially if the manager is found guilty. Don't let authority become misused power and overtake your common sense. You know when you are treating someone wrong. No one has to point it out to you because you know it! You can see it in the employee's face. You hear the comments from other employees. As a manager, it is your responsibility to create a firm but good working environment for everyone. I know . . .

"It's hard being a manager. Somebody's got to do it! Why not me?"

BRINGING OUT
THE WORST

WHEN I HEAR on the news about employees who go into their place of employment (or former employment) trying to kill co-workers, and (in some cases) end up killing their managers, it sends chills up my spine. I always wonder what happened in that work environment. What could cause someone to drive them to do something so extreme?

I can understand the anger but not the intention to kill. I consider myself to be a stable, mentally healthy man but one time I worked for a manager who brought out the worst in me.

Initially, everything seemed to be going well. It was a small organization with no more than 1,000 employees. The bulk of us were housed in one building. I suddenly began to notice that I was being treated differently than my co-workers. My boss seemed to criticize everything I was doing. It really got bad. I found myself reviewing my work over and over again. I even asked my co-workers to review my work before I submitted it to my boss. This made no difference as each and every time my work was being seen as poor quality. I can remember getting depressed as I got closer to the building before I started my day and the headaches I experienced whenever I was called into the manager's office. I would go home and talk about this person and I suddenly realized that my family and friends thought that "I" was the problem. They just did not or could not believe that I was being treated so badly.

To compensate, I started working long hours. I watched everybody leave to go home but I stayed because I wanted to make sure I gave everything I could. My manager would stop by my door and say, "Oh, are you working late again?" I could hear the sarcasm in their voice. Yet, I would force a smile on my face and say, "I won't be here much longer."

As usual, when it was time to review my projects, they were heavily criticized and I was put down (professionally) in the presence of my peers.

. . . . What is painful for me may never cause for an emotion to be raised in others, but right now, I am sitting at my computer looking out my window and I had to stop writing about this segment. My mind started drifting back to when I worked at this particular company and I am feeling the pain all over again. I keep thinking that maybe I should not tell you about this hurtful time in my life and how I almost lost reality. But, I want you to know and understand that we are all human and, if it happened to me, it can happen to you.

I continued to deal with this person to the best of my ability. I felt that as long as I showed them how hard I was working and the excessive time that I was putting into the projects, that ultimately things would get better. I was concerned about my salary because at the time, I had small children who relied on me so when it was time for our pre evaluation and I was rated low, even though I could prove otherwise, it did not matter because I knew and convinced myself that I was being mistreated. I had a choice to make and I decided to take the high road and began to put in longer hours than ever before when one day my boss complimented my work. I was shocked but it made me feel good and I started to feel more confident about what I was doing in my position. I mean, it really felt good to not be the center of attention any longer.

The time came to find out how much of an increase we would get. That particular year, the company had done well and we could get up to 8%. I figured that I would not get the full increase of 8% but I expected to get no less than 3%. It was my turn to be called into the office and my manager started out talking about my performance. Even though they watched me put in long hours, and they had seen some improvement it was not good enough from their perspective and I was told that, *'the company had done well and, they were extremely pleased to give me a 1.5% increase'*. It was at that very moment that I knew that I was losing it.

As I sat there, even though I was looking my boss straight in the face, I was no longer able to listen, or indeed, hear what was being said to me. I could feel the heat inside of me swelling up. My heart started pounding. All I could think about was how small I felt at that moment. I felt humiliated and miss-used. All I could see was the smirk on the manager's face that was clearly sending me a message that, *"I got you"*. When asked if I had any questions, all I could say was, *"no"* I even had the nerve to say, *"thank you"* as I got up from my seat.

I walked back into my office in a state of shock. As I closed the door to sit down at my desk, I could feel tears running down my face. All I could think to say to myself over and over and over was, *"You fool."* Instantly, the hurt turned to anger.

I wanted to go into that office in a rage. I sat looking out my window not realizing that it was going on 6:00 p.m. The meeting had ended almost two hours previous. I didn't tell anybody about what happened to me that day. I had the entire weekend to think about what I was going to do and I started making plans on how I was going to establish my disappointment and anger at the manager and if the worse can to the worse, I would lose my job and start over.

The weekend started and I was still consumed with anger when a friend of mine asked me to attend church with her on Sunday morning. I went and it felt like the minister was preaching directly to me. I cried and cried because I was full of so much anger. I really thank God because had it not been for Him, you probably would not be reading this book right now. I prayed and asked God for strength and to give me peace. I asked God to help me deal with this person. I never would have thought that I could have been so consumed with such rage. I am convinced that based on my spiritual upbringing and my Faith in God that I was able to deal with this situation

The next morning I went into work with a different attitude. I had decided to continue to work hard and was hopeful that things would get better. This person continued to act very unprofessional towards me but I took it. The next week, I received a call from a lady I had interviewed with and she offered me a position paying me substantially more than what I was earning. Man, God is good! The rest is history because from there my career sky-rocketed.

It is very important that as a manager, you must learn to treat ALL employees with equal respect. There will always be various levels of workers in the work environment. Your role is to understand and to think about what you are doing. How are you coming across as a manager? Are you being perceived as supportive, caring and effective, or are you seen as being mean, silly and spiteful. Think about it! I know . . .

"It's hard being a manager. Somebody's got to do it! Why not me?"

ARE YOU DOING THE RIGHT THING WHEN YOU DISCIPLINE?

THIS IS FOR those of you who as managers love to discipline employees. You are too quick to want to write someone up for poor work performance. You are determined to rid yourself of these problem employees. When managers come to me and state that they wish to terminate an employee, the first question I ask is have you done your due diligence. I see and hear the frustration from the manager when I do not support their decision. What they need to appreciate is that I learned the hard way, but you don't have to.

While working at this one particular company, I remember one of the managers having a problem with an employee who was a very poor performer. The manager would come to my office and tell me how she counseled the employee to no avail. A couple of weeks later, I found out that the employee had been suspended for repeated poor work performance. The manager would come to my office and talk about how the suspension was handled by the employee. Finally, the employee was terminated for poor work performance.

Around two months later, we received a letter from the Equal Employment Opportunity Commission (EEOC). This employee alleged discrimination based on race and was alleging wrongful termination. When we asked the manager to provide us with the documentation supporting their decision to terminate the employee, we heard a nightmare. Not only did the manager not have the proper documentation, we discovered that the so called counseling she had with the employee was really impromptu discussions. I learned a great lesson that day.

From that day on, and regardless of the employer, whenever a manager asks to have HR support a termination, I tell the manager that we must pass the Alpha Test.

The reason why I call it the Alpha Test is because it is the beginning of the discipline process and consists of five very important questions.

Here are the Alpha questions:

- Did you sit the employee down and ask if they fully understand their job function?
- If the employee responded with, "Yes, I understand my job function." did you ask the employee to explain back to you their job functions particularly those areas where you have a concern?
- If you were pleased with their response, did you ask the employee if they are aware that they have not been performing well?
- If the employee is not aware, did you go over every aspect of the poor work performance and make sure that the employee clearly understood what you stated and your expectations?
- Did you DOCUMENT the entire meeting and have the employee sign the document prior to the employee leaving your office?

If the answer is NO to ANY of the questions above, I do not support the termination.

If the employee responds clearly and lets you know that they understand every aspect of their job (they articulate it to you better than you expected), this will let you know that maybe there is a misunderstanding in that you don't feel they are performing well but the employee believes that they are doing a decent job. Essentially, the employee is unaware of their poor performance and may as a result of some self evaluation process truly believe that they are doing better than ever before.

When you tell them your concerns and they show no response and refuse to sign anything then, you do the Omega Test. I call it the Omega Test because these questions help you to understand what the end result may be if you answer no to any of these questions,

Here are the Omega questions:

- Have you reviewed their last three performance evaluations?
- Has this employee ever been disciplined?
- Have you treated this employee the same way you treat your other employees?

- Did you inform your superior about this employee and are they in agreement that they may need to be disciplined?
- Are you ready to take on this challenge until the very end?

If you have answered no to any of these questions, the end result will be a win for the employee and frustration for management. I don't like looking at it as a win or lose situation but (as the young kids say) *"It is what it is!"* The Omega Test helps you to get prepared for the battle, and it is a battle. You have to turn all of the Omega Test questions from a no to a yes. Once you can respond with a yes to each of these questions, you are ready to begin your behavior correction process with this employee.

It is unrealistic to think that as a manager it is not your responsibility to make sure that you have done your job effectively. I have discovered that one area that managers struggle to deal with is discipline. If you really think about the Alpha Test, it allows the manager to approach a problem employee with concern, patience, and understanding. Why? Because if the employee responds with a, *"No, I don't fully understand my job function,"* this gives you the opportunity to educate and train the employee in the way you want them to do their job. I know, some employees play a game and say, no they don't understand, when they really do understand. In these instances, the employees (from what I have seen) always end up terminated faster than you think.

Don't ever assume that employees really know how to do their job. Play it safe and give the Alpha Test. You will be surprised at what you may hear. I know . . .

"It's hard being a manager. Somebody's got to do it! Why not me?"

KEEPING CONTROL

THE MENTALITY OF some of the employees entering the workplace today is simply amazing to me. They act like they don't have a clue about what they are doing wrong. I have sat in on disciplinary meetings and watched the employees get an attitude with the manager because an issue or concern was brought to their attention seeking improvement. When I say they got an attitude, I mean they were down right angry.

Once I sat in on a meeting for an employee who had an excessive attendance problem. She was late for work ninety percent of the time. That means she was coming into work late, four out of five days per week. When management finally got tired and had to address the issue, the employee became extremely irate. After much discussion, the employee refused to sign the warning and felt that she was being harassed. Can you believe it? The employee turned the tables on the manager and accused them of harassment. I watched as the manager began to act nervous and started defending herself as to why the employee was not being harassed by management. By the time the meeting ended, the employee walked out without the warning and the manager was angry and frustrated. The manager allowed the employee to take control of the meeting.

As a manager, it is important to always maintain control when you are meeting with your employees. Not control in the sense of no one can speak unless you give them permission. The type of control that I am suggesting is when the employee tries to place you on the defensive and you find yourself defending who you are as a manager. In this example, the manager did not stay focused on the reason for calling the meeting and the outcome she was seeking. Instead, she gave this employee the opportunity to question management skills. I did not intervene during this meeting because it is very important that this and every manager learn how to manage effectively and the only way that a manager can do this is to learn from mistakes, so I let this meeting play itself out. I also knew that based on the attendance record of this employee, it would be a matter of time before the manager would have to address their attendance again.

So please remember when calling a meeting to address an issue or concern, it is your responsibility to maintain control of the meeting. If the employee wishes to bring up issues or concerns (which may be very valid) state to the employee, "You have raised a valid point. Let's discuss it." Once you have discussed their issues or concerns and it has not changed your decision, go back into the reason for the meeting and proceed. If what they stated gives you reason to rethink your decision, inform the employee that you will need to do an investigation. As the manager, you have used diplomacy without behaving in a weak manner. Do you get it? You must always maintain control and never ever let an employee believe they have control over you. I know . . .

"It's hard being a manager. Somebody's got to do it! Why not me?"

STROKING

DO YOU STROKE your employees? Maybe you don't know what stroke means. It means, do you praise your employees and let them know of the great job they are doing? Everybody needs to be stroked by somebody. I need it! It is important to me and for me when my superior gives me a compliment relating to my job. It's like an adrenaline rush. It does something to your self esteem. In many ways we are our own worse enemy. We judge ourselves harder than others. We look at our own mistakes and take them to another level. I used to find myself beating my self up then out of nowhere my boss would say to me how well I was performing. Now think about it. At my level as a senior in HR, if I am overwhelmed to hear a positive response, how do you think a lower level employee will feel when being complimented by their supervisor or manager? You must stroke all of your employees at some point in time, even the ones that are not performing well. When they do something right you should compliment them on whatever it may be. The goal is, if you stroke them on the little things eventually, they will get the picture and a snow ball effect of improved work performance will be established. There will always be those who, regardless of what you say to them, don't care and will show no emotions. I recommend you stroke them anyway. Eventually, they will say thank you. At least I hope they will. I know . . .

"It's hard being a manager. Somebody's got to do it! Why not me?"

SUPPORT WHERE YOU WORK

I DO NOT UNDERSTAND how someone who is working as the manager of an organization does not support the product of the organization. Here you are working in a hospital but you tell friends and family don't ever take you to that hospital for service. Everyday you work in a mega store but you tell folks that you go to the competition for your products. Do you get the picture? I don't understand this type of thinking. It is totally unacceptable to work for an organization, let them pay for your health care and provide you with a steady paycheck to support your lifestyle, but you talk about them in the worst type of way. You owe that organization (if nothing else) a few positive words when someone asks you about where you work. Even if you don't like your employer, there is a way to say something that does not give the person the wrong impression.

When I hear non management employees speak negatively about their employer, I don't like it. But when a manager (someone who has said that I want to take on more responsibility and manage other people) engages in the same foolish conversation as their support staff, it is disheartening. As a manager, you should know the mission and the goals of the organization. You should always be prepared to talk about the mission to your employees. In every staff meeting, you should discuss the yearly goals and why they are important. You must educate your staff continuously to ensure they are in sync with the mission and goals of the organization.

Remember, if your employees hear you speaking negatively about the organization, they will do and say the same as you. There will be times when you need to vent your frustrations. The place for you to do this is in a peer meeting or with your boss. Someplace where you can be heard and possibly see some of your suggestions being implemented. Remember, it's the way you say it that matters the most. I know . . .

"It's hard being a manager. Somebody's got to do it! Why not me?"

AND FINALLY

ALL THINGS MUST come to an end. I can see the smile on your face if you have gotten this far. Why I see that smile without physically being next to you is because I am smiling.

I hope I have given you a healthy snap shot in to the world of management. There are many authors out there and hundreds of books on management but my goal is to make the reading fun and easy to understand through a simple book that you can pick up and read as a reminder and have as a management tool for reinforcement on a daily basis. I am sincere for you to have learned something about management that has never been taught to you, or it has been taught to you in such a way that you did not comprehend it fully until you read my book. Clearly, I don't know everything about management, but, I believe if you try a few of my suggestions you will make a difference in how you manage.

I know that being a manager is hard. Somebody's got to do it. Why not me?

This is a very sincere statement. It could be and should be you. Don't feel apprehensive about working in the world of management, it pays well and provides you with plenty of opportunity and growth. More importantly, it allows you to lead as a "Change Agent".

It is my wish that you have learned or decided whether or not management is the right place for you. I know that it is hard being in management. Anytime you have the ability to tell other folks how to do their job, it's a challenge. It is very time consuming, demanding, and it can be frustrating. Yet, it can be, exciting, creative, satisfying, innovative and rewarding. To have the opportunity to help bring about change in any organization is exciting. Not many people get the opportunity to work in the capacity of a manager. If you are approached or have the opportunity to work in management, don't be afraid. Don't let others talk you out of it because it means you are going to change and become somebody different. You remain the same but your actions and perceptions of how you see things will change and through this you will grow.

I've heard some managers refer to management (particularly front line or middle management) as a dumping ground. Every and anything that has to be done is dumped on them. They "catch hell" from Senior Leadership and they "catch hell" from their employees. This may be true in some cases, but, if you take the time to really internalize the topics I have brought to your attention, you can survive.

MOVING ON

L AST BUT NOT least, know when it is time to move on. There are several layers of management. Each layer brings you closer and closer to your ultimate goal. It is natural and healthy to want to grow, so once the job has become so routine that you don't enjoy what you do, it is time to move on

I would love to hear from you, your comments about my thoughts and opinions. Please send your comments to my email address. Remember,

"It's hard being a manager. Somebody's got to do it! Why not me?"

ABOUT THE AUTHOR

H.R. SCOTT has always considered himself an HR junkie. He loves the profession of Human Resources Management and he has a passion for providing management with the right tools to do their job effectively.

The passion he has regarding Human Resource Management is unbelievable until you hear him speak. H.R. Scott has lived what he is marketing to others, his words are immensely motivating. His own career has been filled with excitement, anger, and frustration, yet, H.R. Scott continued to persevere because he knew there is a message out there for others to hear.

H.R. Scott is available for consultation and speaking engagements. You may contact him at his email address, rscotthr@yahoo.com or you may call him at (510) 301-3172.